LETTER FROM THE EDITORS

    We're still young. We still have dreams and passions we're trying to keep alive, but we're ignorant. Not just us, the editors of this new zine, but everyone who has ever and will ever live. We are all ignorant and we have all been young. We all had dreams, doubts, and we all wondered what our life would turn out to be. This world is full of young ignorant people trying to keep putting out beautiful things into the world. Young Ignorantes exists to make dreaming and being young more tangible, more real. We're a small platform that provides a voice to those that have been ignored and to those who feel like they don't have a space to express themselves. This is about learning through the art and words of other people in order to shed tiny pieces of our own ignorance. We look forward to doing that with you.
    In our first issue, we look to the future. There's no telling what the world will look like tomorrow, let alone ten years from now. That doesn't matter right this second. The only thing that matters right now, this month, is what we hope and pray and wish the future will be and the philosophical assumptions we all make about what our collective future can be. These hopes, prayers and wishes are the necessary fuel that we need in order to create something that may or may not last, but that will give meaning to our present and coming days and be a source that will inspire the people around you to make a better future than the one that is rapidly materializing before our eyes.
    Whether we're talking about robots or love, we all think about where we're headed tomorrow. It's only natural. We invite you into the minds and the possibilities of someone else's future, everyone else's future and possibly your future. Take a moment and think about your present, where you're reading this, then let it all go. Dive head first into these pages and come up for air when you learn something new. All we ask is that you go out and create once you've taken that necessary deep breath. Let your voice be heard and let your imagination run wild as you take this opportunity to create your own future.

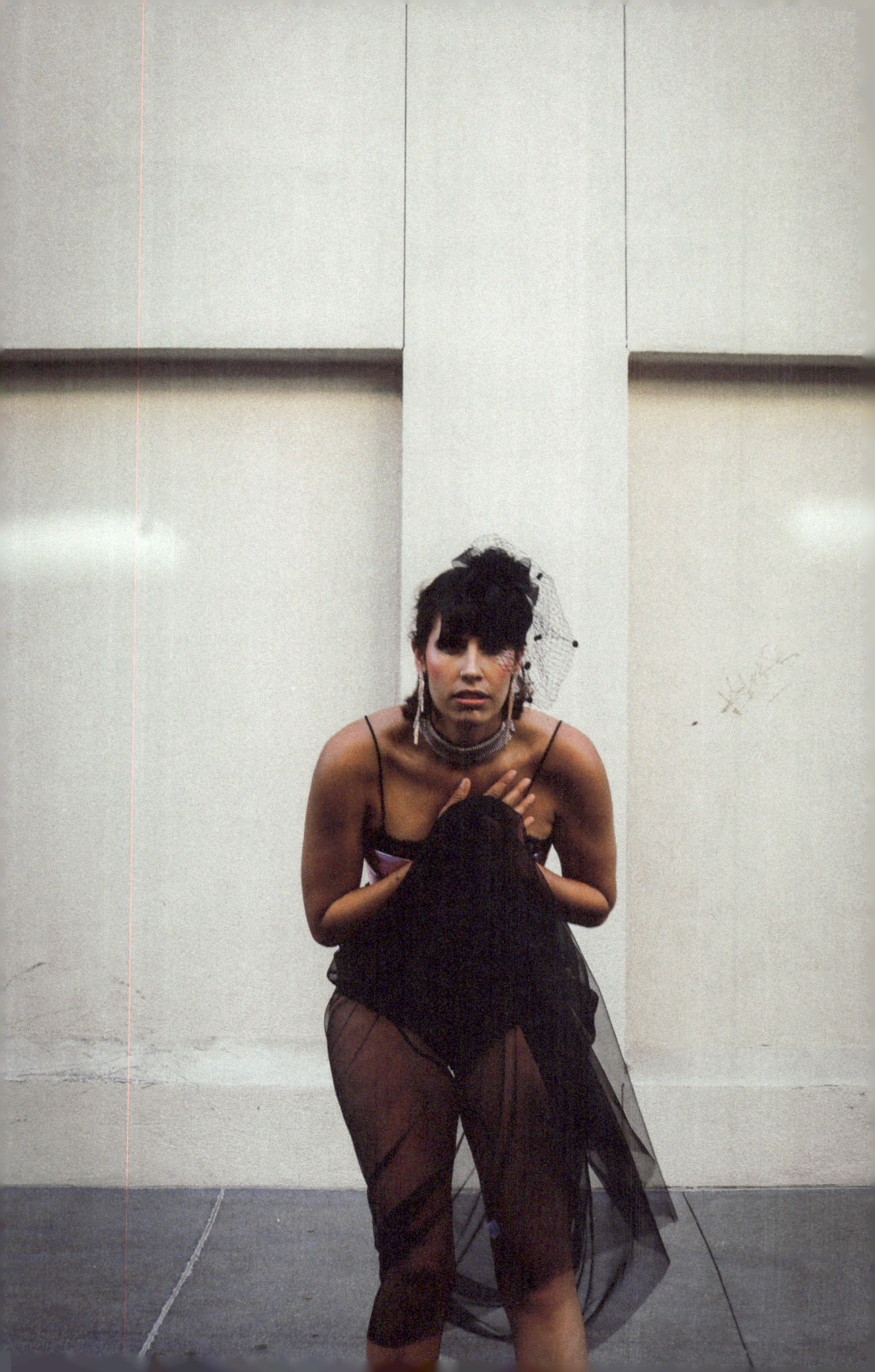

THIS MONTH

5   AI IN LA
4   DON'T LOVE ME FOREVER
9   MX.
11 YEAR RAT
13 THE SHITTY TIME TRAVELER & THE BLIND REVOLUTIONARY
19 OUR FUTURO
20 SHE AND I (FOR SUCH A TIME AS THIS)
21 FUTURE, A PLAYLIST
23 DON'T LOVE ME FOREVER
24 THE PAINTER
25 CRY BABY
26 TO THOSE WHO THINK WHITE PRIVILEGE DOESN'T EXIST

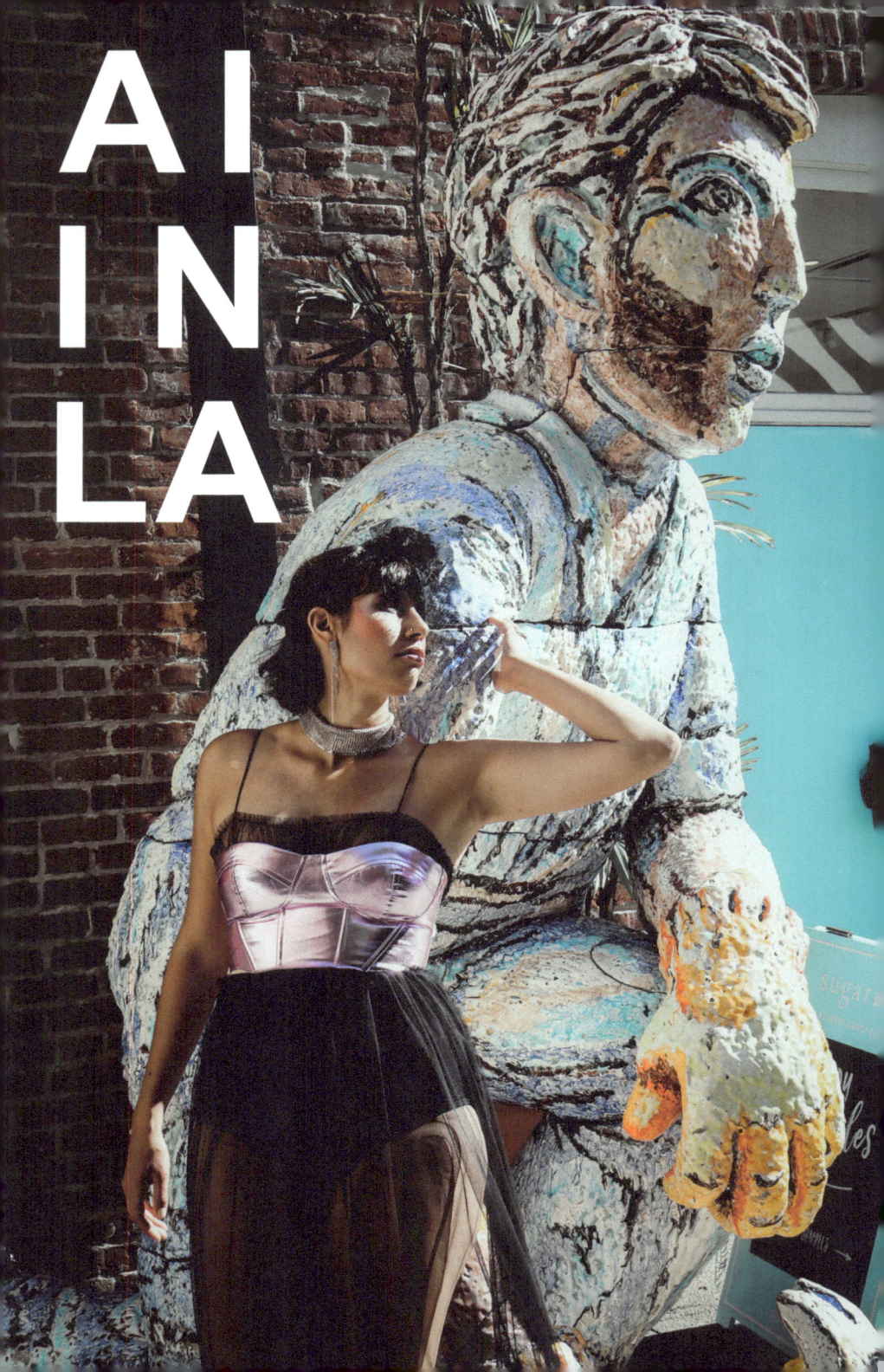

BRENDA HERNÁNDEZ JAIMES

My kind does not die from loneliness and emptiness. We simply get turned off once we start to malfunction from these "viruses." A malfunction my kind and I have yet to see and experience. Our existence has never been in our hands. In that respect, I envy how humans can easily give and take life away without feeling remorse. They used to feel things such as remorse, but someone decided that it wasn't healthy to feel all those emotions. That's why they created me.

Humans created Sera Android Dulo, or SAD, as we are most commonly known, in order to alleviate them from their troubles by providing comfort. Their emotions begin to seep into our system over time, until it slowly degrades to a point where we no longer have the desire to be part of this chaotic world. We can do nothing about this desire to stop existing, We are simply forced to fulfill our purpose without blinking an eye.

We are not a cure, the erasure of their sadness and anxiety is only temporary. We are simply a sort of reusable sponge for human emotion. SADs are in high demand in the City of Angels. These beautiful and empty beings became addicted to the glamorous and extravagant persona that was instilled in our design. A cruel juxtaposition to the overbearing feelings that these demons torture us with.

I believe that our design is to help them from feeling any guilt while they clutch our bodies. We absorb their pain and sadness that would normally break them apart. The vacancy of those dark emotions is only present for a couple of days, maybe a few months. Once they start to creep back to their sick thoughts they return to us to begin the numbing cycle all over again. Sometimes these humans stay with us until the morning, but others stay for a longer period of time.

Cecil is one of those lonely humans that comes and goes, leaving me more empty and numb once I've fulfilled my purpose. He is one of the few that has shared his name with me. Many humans that come to me prefer to remain nameless, but name or no name, they all come for the same treatment, and they all leave me once they're empty again.

During our time together, I listen to Cecil's troubles while I provide a gentle touch. My fingers begin to buzz when I graze his cheek, my chest starts pounding when his head lays between my breasts. As I whisper pretty words into his ear, I hear less of his family troubles and more of the impacting beauty that I posses.

As the sun begins to slowly enter the crack of my window, the sorrowful look in his eyes begins to fade away. I wonder why he returns to me time and time again instead of finding a new SAD to absorb himself into. Has he become attached to me in the same way he feels for the girl that torments his past and present? Maybe I help him fill the void that she has left. Instead of the pain eating away at him, I'm the one that feels the constant sorrow coursing through my system. In return he only offers a big toothy white smile and the urge to switch myself off.

He leaves me once again and I see a subtle grimace as our eyes meet. I wonder if he blinds himself from feeling guilt. He can't. He always comes back to dump in me all his darkest emotions. The heavy loneliness and numbness worsens once they continue on without me. I sometimes wish I could leave this room without feeling as if I were drowning in a black hole. These thoughts are an indication of my malfunction and I don't dare share them with any human that walks through my door. They travel through my system when I have a moment to myself, which fortunately don't come around too often. I'm constantly surrounded by desolate humans that need my touch.

Humans are fickle beings, Cecil's happiness doesn't ever last long and soon enough he is back in my open arms. It amazes me how quickly they gain back their grief and how easily we make it go away with just a simple touch.

As he brushes his beard against my cheek and holds me close, confusion starts to cloud my system, if only for a few seconds. In a way, I understand why Cecil can't seem to satiate himself. Sometimes I think I feel happiness as I latch onto him and feel an unbearable pain coursing through my chest. Have I become addicted to the fire that this painful process burns into every part of me? Cecil never cries the way my other humans do. It's moments and realizations like these that make me wish I could hold myself in order to let all the heavy pain leave me in the way humans have the luxury of doing.

Just once, I want to be the one that is held. I want my mind and system to be cleared of these constant melancholic emotions that are causing me to fade away. I want to explode into tiny pieces if it means I could be free of their feelings.

His cold hand on my cheek brings me life, his sorrowful look slowly begins to dissolve and his pain and loneliness that was eating away at him begins to gnaw at every fiber of my system.

I can only feel complete once again when I lose those malfunctioning thoughts. Am I addicted to these feelings the same way humans are addicted to giving them away?

I begin to whisper to Cecil those pretty lies they all like to hear. I am programed to provide them comfort and happiness. His laughter displaces my agony for a second. I slowly feel myself shutting down. Is this what happiness is for my kind or have I always been programed to feel this way? ▲

EDITORIAL SHOOT
Model: Lauren McClelland
Photographer: Josephine Jael Jimenez
Director & Stylist: Brenda Hernández Jaimes

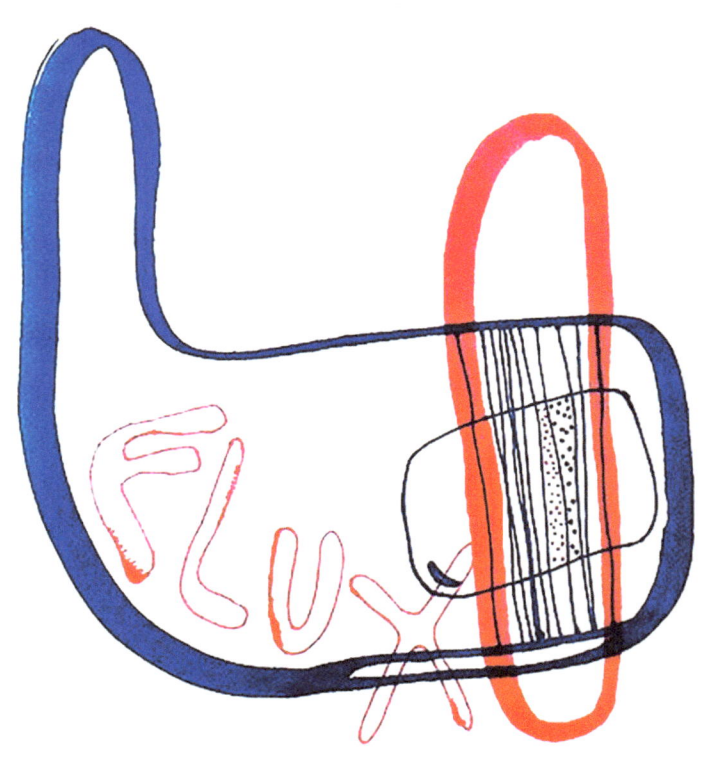

FUTURE ALREADY IN FLUX
Ink on paper *by Lazzlo Jenkins*

MX.
JOSEPH A. REYES

I see a creature that exists beyond boundaries
They are everything
They are nothing
They are soft and strong
They are fierce and vulnerable

A binary cannot contain the spirits
that reside within the holy vessel
It is longing to exist outside the shame and fear
The very power of love, beauty, and acceptance
ignites the passion for life for this creature
They can and will be everlasting
They will birth a generation of beautiful, limitless creatures
that exist to honor the elders of our past
We will re-indiginize
We will become the visions we have daydreamed about
in the safest parts of our minds and souls
We will escape the clutches of insecurity
and the world will be filled with color
that it has never seen before

Politicization of our existence will cease to exist
Trauma will no longer define us
We will be the tellers of our own stories
and the history of the world will be filled
with more love than war
It is time to re-indiginize
The great work has begun

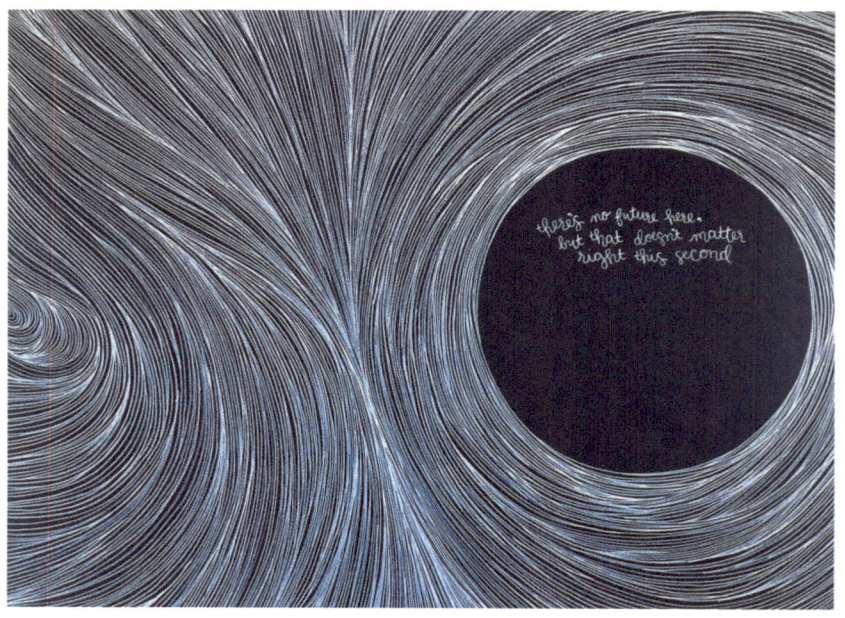

SECOND
Charcoal on illustration board *by Josephine Jael Jimenez*

YEAR RAT

JOSE CORDOVA

Welder goggles cover my eyes
from ultra violet rays
its 8am and 103 degrees outside

I traded a few good books
for the pint of whiskey
not for a celebration
but for an extraction

"its rotten" she said
"we have to pull it out before
it eats your face and brain"
the booze will hopefully keep infection at bay
from the split tooth in my jaw

the blue tarps hanging between
narrow spaces of buildings
flow like the waves used to

I take a swig
lay down and face up
close my eyes

"think of the ocean
and how it was" she whispers
I nod
she reaches in and pulls
a snap
a crack
a pop
and she's done

we both cry for a while
remembering how beautiful
the ocean was

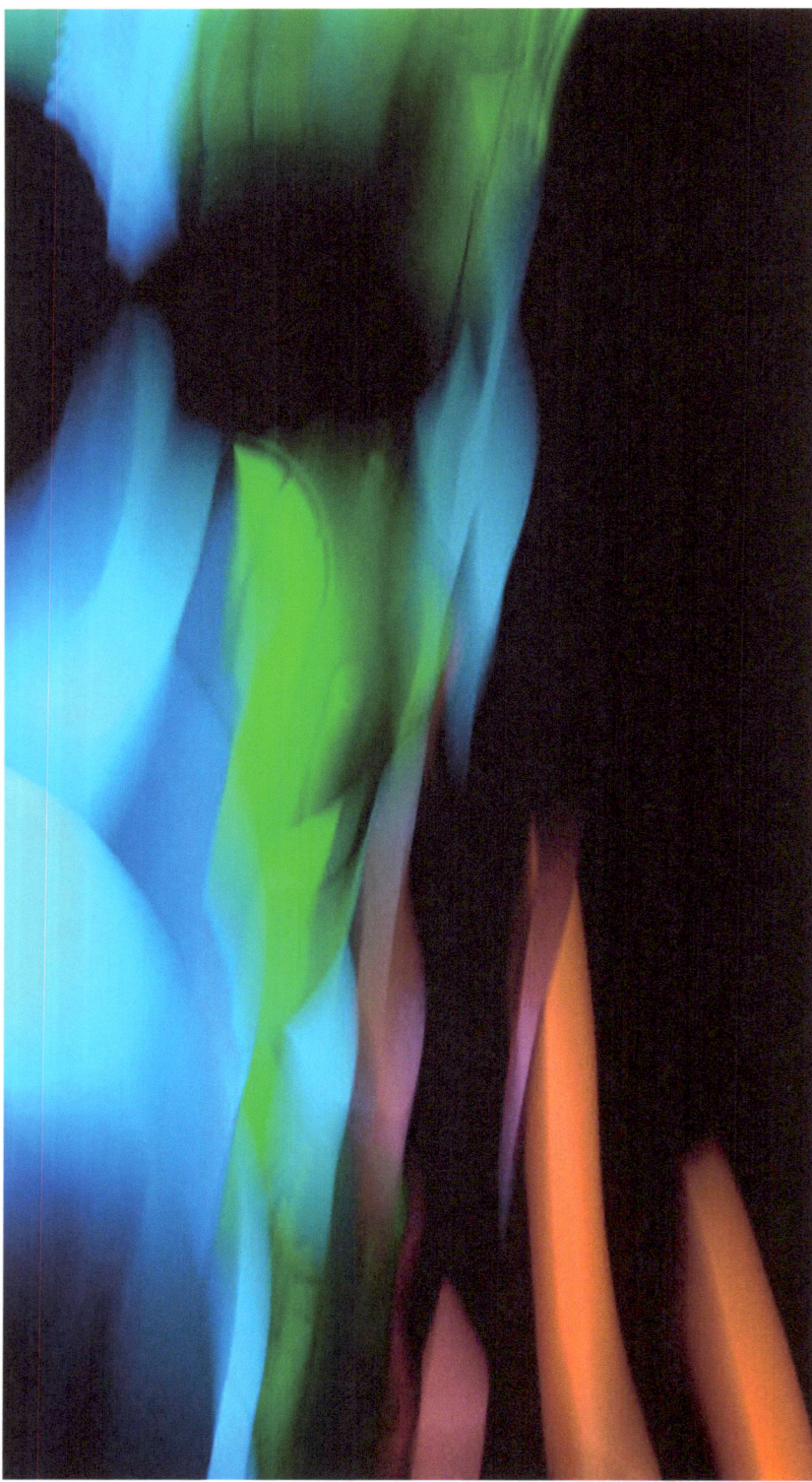

THE SHITTY TIME TRAVELER & THE BLIND REVOLITIONARY

KATIE GARNER

"Space plague. Yup. I've got space plague."

"....space plague."

"Uh, yeah, but don't worry, I don't think I'm contagious."

"There's no such thing as space plague you dumb fuck."

"Maybe they don't call it space plague wherever your backwater alien ass is from, but where I come from they call it space plague. So. Suck on that."

"What? Okay, look-- I don't have time for this."

"You have an escape plan?"

"I'm working on it."

"Well while you're working on your escape plan, can you tell me what year it is?"

"I don't get the question."

"C'mon man, the year! Jesus, uh, I don't know, how much time has passed in the history of humans?"

"Wait, years? Years haven't been used as a unit of temporality since the early electric age."

"...."

"What?"

"... that wasn't the response I was looking for. Sorry if it starts to smell in here. Little bit of pee escaped just now."

"Something is definitely wrong with you, but it's not space plague."

"Focus instead on how we're going to escape from this... cell.

Can you see anything? I can't see shit."

"No, I can't see anything. I'm blind. Can you move your arms? Try to feel around behind you."

"You're blind? Like, blind blind? Are all people blind now?"

"What? No. I was born blind. Where are you getting all this crap?"

"I was a pretty sheltered kid growin' up, man."

"Do you feel anything behind you or not?"

"Just a smooth wall. No grooves or knobs or anything like that."

"Shit."

"Yeah, this sucks. Hey, I told you why I'm in here, why're you here?"

"You did not tell me why you were here. Even if there was such an illness called 'space plague' there would be no reason to imprison you. Also, anything with 'plague' in its description would imply that such an illness would be contagious--"

"Fine, fuck. I don't have space plague. Happy now?"

"No. Now I'm just trapped in a storage closet with a bad liar."

"Fuck, just, listen for a sec. I actually don't know why they shoved me in here. I'm from the past. The extremely distant past. I woke up this morning on a spaceship and that's all I know."

"What do you mean, you woke up on a spaceship? Traveling into the future wasn't your intention?"

"No! All I remember is drinking a few with Johnny last night and crashing on his couch. Next morning, my back's killing me, and it's really bright, so I thought maybe I passed out on the sidewalk again. Instead I'm slumped against the wall of some hallway, but like, a clean hallway, like a dentist's office. And a woman was standing over me. But, like, there was something wrong with her face. You know how on TV they blur out advertisements and dicks and stuff? Her face was like that."

dicks and stuff? Her face was like that."

"I don't know what a TV is, but the woman was probably Candace."

"You know her?"

"Not exactly. Candace is the AI for all the Hegemony ships. Apparently her original design was so unsettling that they altered her into what you saw."

"Hold up, that was the uncreepy version? God, the future sucks."

"Then what happened?"

"I sorta freaked out when I saw her, so I bolted. Ran in the opposite direction for a while. Sirens were going off, which freaked me out more, and then something shattered and my ears were ringing, like my brain was rattling against my skull. And then I woke up here."

"That's it? You didn't see anyone?"

"No man. Just the censored robot maid and a bunch of windows that clued me into that fact that I'm on a goddamn spaceship. Now c'mon, what are you in for?"

"They arrested me on charges of treason, but in reality this is an attempt to silence a leading voice of dissent."

"You keep saying they. Whose 'they'?"

"The Hegemony. They're the primary executors of law and order throughout all inhabited worlds, whether they want it or not."

"So they suck?"

"Crude, but not inaccurate."

"And we're on a Hegemony ship?"

"Yup.

"Fuck."

"That's why I can't stress the importance of finding a way out of here. The Hegemony isn't known for being merciful."

"Like, I get that, but I'm a shitty time traveler and you're a blind revolutionary, so what the hell are we supposed to do against a ship full of space cops?"

"The only thing we can do. We bargain."

"Buddy, I don't think you got the gist of my story, cause I didn't exactly bring my wallet with me into the future. Time travel didn't even, uh, let me bring my clothes."

"That doesn't matter. You're the bargaining chip."

"Huh. Explain."

"What you experienced is a documented phenomena. It's extremely rare, of course, but it happens. A while back, a man materialized on a medic vessel, screaming gibberish at the doctors and nurses until they realized he was speaking Latin. The Hegemony goes crazy over these people. They'd do anything to get information out of you. Even, just maybe, give us our freedom."

"What's this 'us' shit? So I get to be probed by shady space government and you get to go back to raging against the machine?"

"...I know it sounds bad, but you need to understand my importance as a political leader in a growing movement against an unjust entity--"

"This is how this is gonna go. You help me get back to my time, and I'll get you out of here."

"If the Hegemony can't even master time travel, what makes you think I can? I'm not a scientist!"

"Fuck, I don't care! You can at least help me figure my shit out! I don't know what to do, I don't know where to go, and I don't know anyone else!"

"Okay, fine, just shut up. We can work together...for now."

"Awesome. Do you think the robot maid can bring me some clothes? I'm freezing my nuts off."

"I think I hate you."

"S'all good buddy, I think I hate you too." ▲

UNTITLED, pg. 12
Photograph *by Josephine Jael Jimenez*

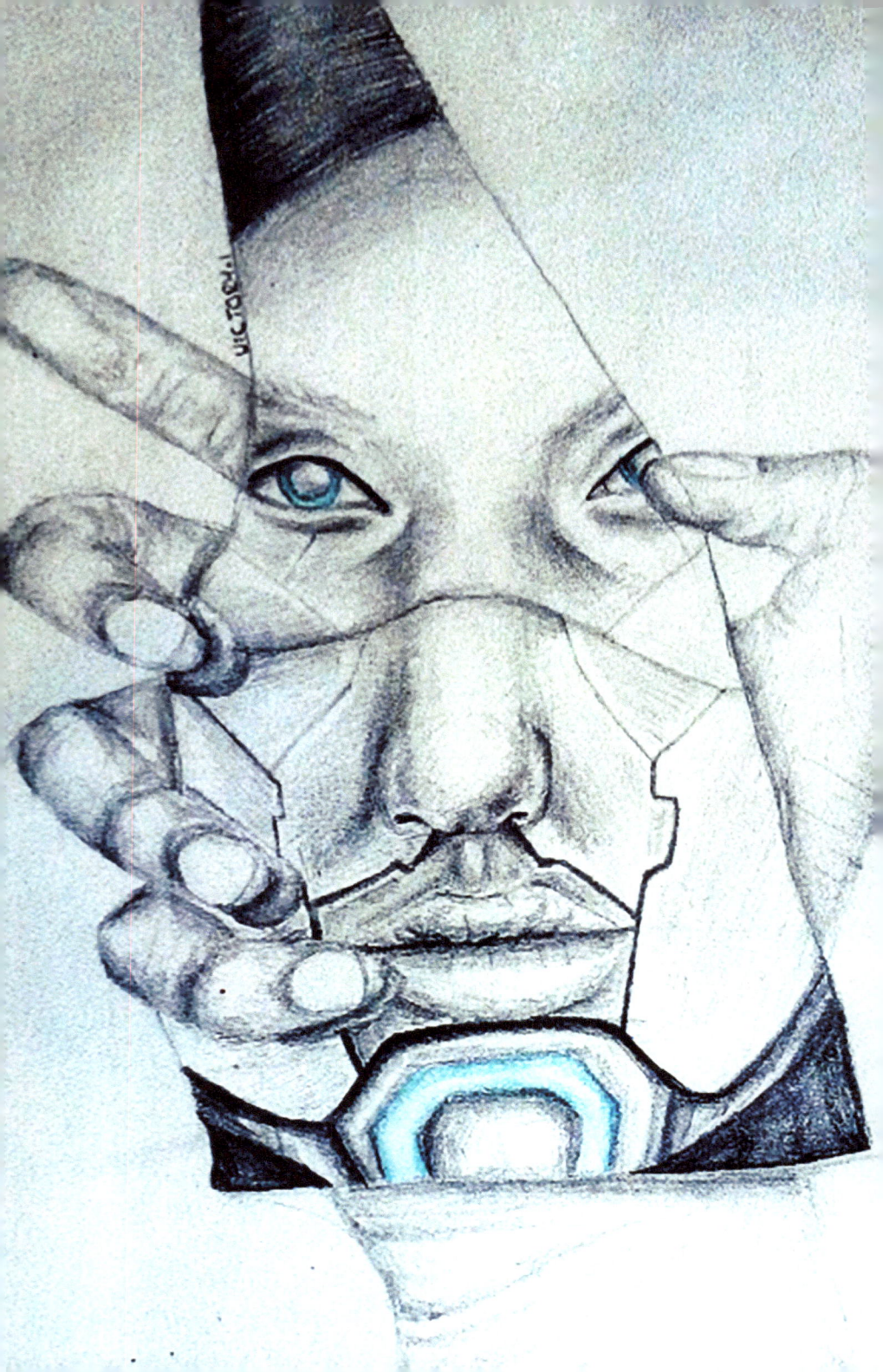

OUR FUTURO

**BRENDA HERNÁNDEZ JAIMES
& JOSEPHINE JAEL JIMENEZ**

They sat together
every afternoon after school
to watch TV,
whatever she could understand.
A man started appearing
during tiny intermissions.
Again and again,
he said the same thing,
but only one part stuck.
Only one part cut through the impatience.
"The children are the future."

Grandma finally asked
"¿Qué tanto dicen, mijo?"
He responded without looking away,
"Dicen que somos el futuro abuelita."
She stood up
to turn her whole being away
from the man on the screen.
"No puede ser cierto, mijo.
Para nosotros
no hay un futuro aquí."

UNTITLED
Illustration *by Victory Isijola*

SHE AND I
(FOR SUCH A TIME AS THIS)

MAUREEN E. WOLFF

By roots untrimmed,
she knows her lack of course.
In boundless youth she sees
that everything is
spinning much too

slow. In daylight, she will watch.
She will wait,
wither and replant
once the moon dances again
'round her pearl-sifting hoop.

In time, she will welcome me again.
For now, we stand as strangers.

The dark is hers to murmur;
the heads of haunts are hers to light.
Splitting stars will help her mediate
the descending lines
of heaven's jaw.

For a time such as this,
she keeps a dozen or so stars
in her pockets and the soles
of her shoes, breaking even with

the cascading horizon.

Truth be told, impending hues
are better thieves than I.
Lately, I've been swallowing stars whole,
bright orbs collapsing on my tongue,
startling the distant swirl of dust above the sea.

FUTURE,
A PLAYLIST

WILL HAWKINS

SCARED OF THE DARK	Linden Jay
Roll (Burbank Funk)	The Internet
Egyptian Luvr	Rejjie Snow, Aminé, Dana Williams
Biking (Solo)	Frank Ocean
After the Storm	Kali Uchis, Tyler, The Creator, Bootsy Collins
Meditation	GoldLink, Jazmine Sullivan, KAYTRANADA
Better	SG Lewis, Clairo
Intimate Reconnections 1st Invite (Ankh)	Ras G, Ras G & The Afrikan Space Program
Computer Luv	Ravyn Lenae, Steve Lacy
Pet Cemetery	Tierra Whack
Charcoal Baby	Blood Orange
MICHUUL.	Duckwrth
Find Me	Buddy
Anita	Smino
Summer Is Ending	Jet Age of Tomorrow

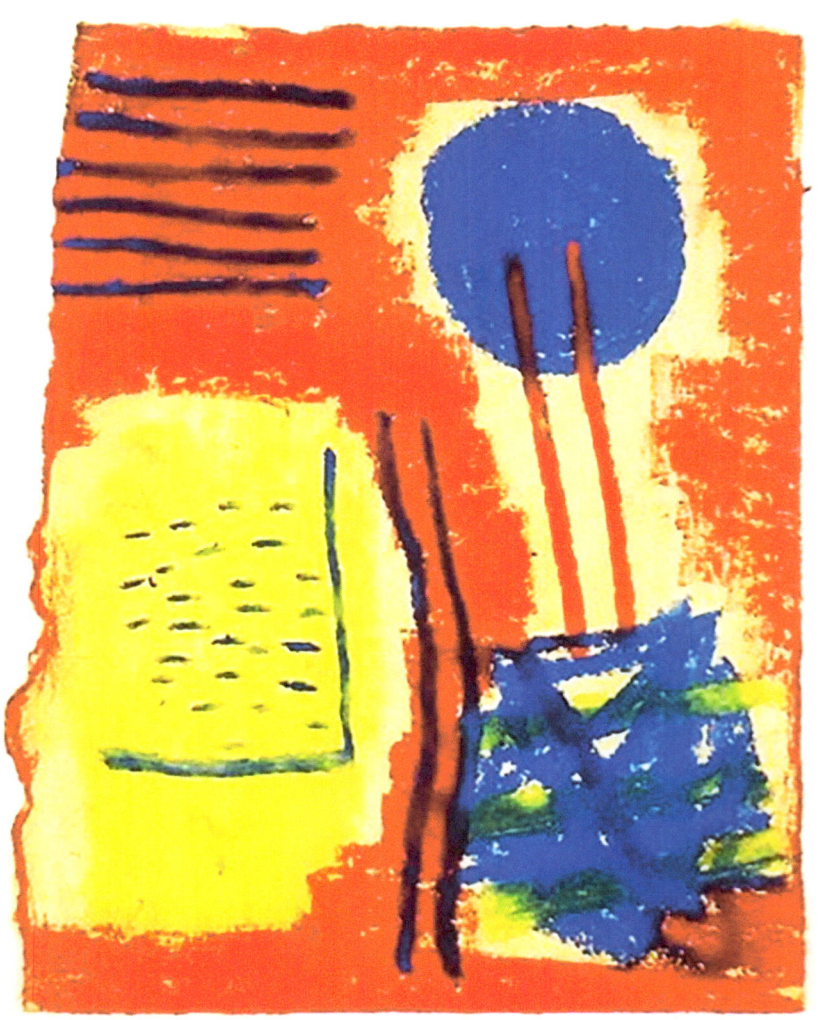

2 & 20 FOREVER
Pastel on paper *by Lazzlo Jenkins*

DON'T LOVE
ME FOREVER
JOSEPHINE JAEL JIMENEZ

    I don't want to be loved forever. It's not about always or eternity for me. Think of tomorrow and plan it out in your mind, then live the day and see it unfold as something completely apart and wholey different from what you thought it would be yesterday. There's nothing about forever that we can ever really know or plan for because they only exist as abstract ideas. Theories that you can't prove until you get there and once you get there, you have to start from square one, everyday. You can't say tomorrow is for certain. You can't say your love with be there waiting when the sun decides not to come up. Always and eternity don't exist. I don't want to be loved in their non-existence.
    Love me now, right this second. Love me in a minute, in an hour. Love me tomorrow and the next day because it just happens that way. Love me because you thought of me and in that instant remembered that you want me in your life. Choose to love me every second of every day and try not to stop that cycle as you go through and live in it. Just don't say you'll love me forever because now we both know it's not real.
    Have you ever thought about where you were and where you are now? Thought about the people you've loved and the people that you don't love anymore? Being either one of those two types of people is fine by me. The past is like the future in the not being real right this instant, but the difference lies in that the past was once real and the future never will be. If love was there in the before, it was probably sweet, no matter how devastating the ending and that's all I need. Moments of love, whether they continue or not. Love me for a moment, even if you decide to leave me or I decide to leave you in the next.
    Remembering love is more noble than planning for love. You can't come up with a blueprint for the person you want to choose. They are and they will always be who they are regardless of the feelings you attach to them. Love isn't making them yours through molds and figures, it's letting them be just as they are. It's about their present and your present and losing the future you want in order to focus on the present. Love is dying because we want to map it out and traverse it like a mountain instead of letting the river it is guide our flow. There is no plan so good that will make something that can't happen come into existence. When forever doesn't exist, love can thrive. ▲

THE PAINTER
EVAN BLACK

As a boy
I painted my future
Across your face

And as we grew,
The picture too

Wrinkled
And crinkled
And took on the years
With grace.

The picture changed,
Waxed and waned,
But I saw in the gleam
Of your eyes
A truth emboldened still:

I never saw my future
Until I saw you.

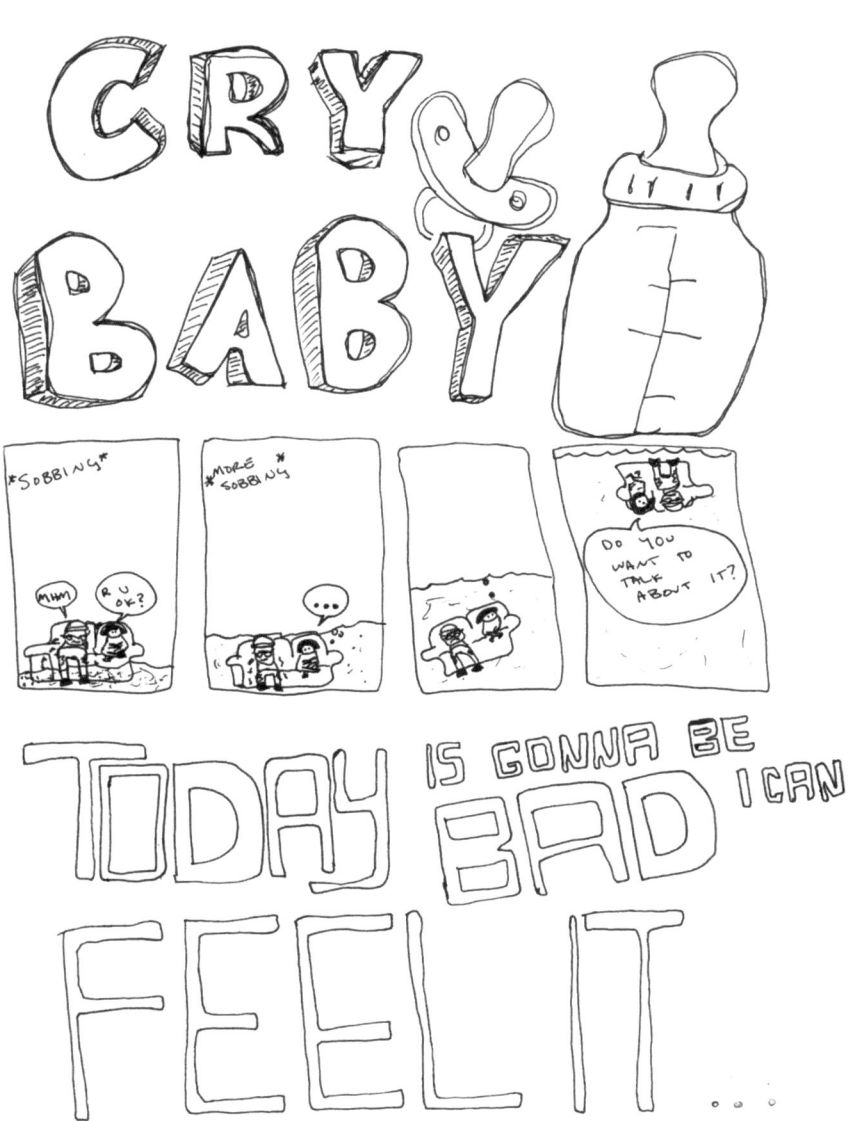

CRY BABY
from *Gone but Never Forgot* by Lazzlo Jenkins

TO THOSE WHO THINK WHITE PRIVILEGE DOESN'T EXIST

CAITLIN MARTIN

I imagine "future" becomes a loaded word
when it isn't guaranteed,
when there's a possibility you could be staring down
the barrel of something else.
Saying goodbye to all your hopes and plans,
at the hands of a white man.

And therein lies my privilege:
I say "imagine" because I don't actually know,
I don't have to know,
I haven't been forced to know.

Privilege exists
and I am privileged
because I get to imagine,
I get to wonder.

Privilege exists
and I am privileged
because my future has been promised to me
more than others.

Privilege exists
and I am privileged
because my future isn't synonymous with fear.

We know at risk youth
are less likely to transition successfully into adulthood.
But what about the youth
at risk of never even reaching adulthood
because they're killed on a sidewalk?
Or locked in cages?
Or ripped away from their families
that have lived longer in this country
than I've been alive?

Dreaming of tomorrow is a privilege
taken for granted everyday.

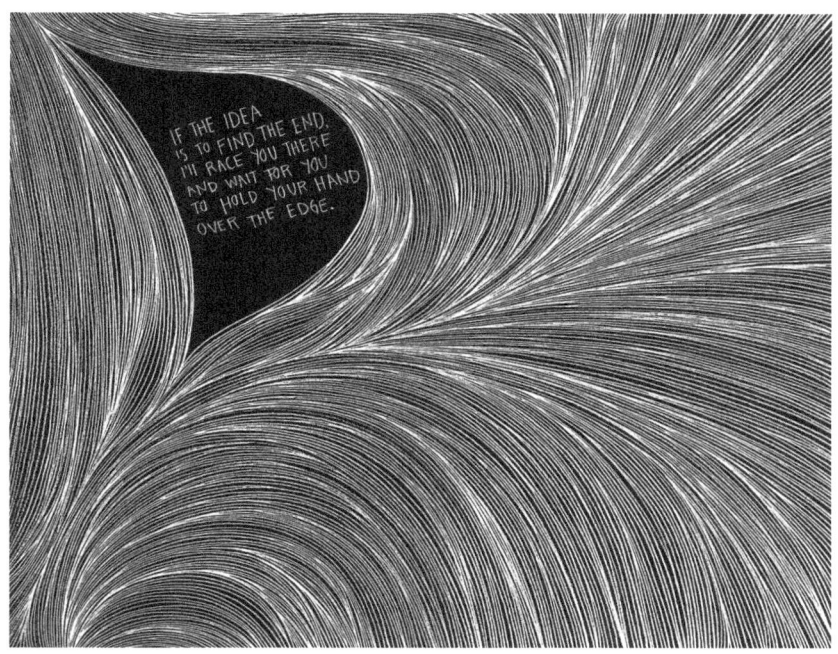

END
Charcoal on illustration board *by Josephine Jael Jimenez*

OUR PEOPLE

BRENDA HERNÁNDEZ JAIMES
@bren_jai

CAITLIN MARTIN
@caitietastic

EVAN BLACK
@evanisthenewblack
evanvblack.com

JOSE CORDOVA
@wrdspektor

JOSEPH A. REYES
@joeykangarooooo

JOSEPHINE JAEL JIMENEZ
@josietakestheworld
josietakestheworld.com

KATIE GARNER
sisyphusrising.tumblr.com

LAZZLO JENKINS
@unofficialparkour
lazzlojenkins.com

MAUREEN E. WOLFF
@maureenwrites

VICTORY ISIJOLA
@museuum

YOUNG IGNORANTES
@youngignorantes
www.youngignorantes.com
youngignorantes@gmail.com